AMO A MI HOODIE

Escrito por
Isreba Aiken
"TCC"
Hope Syndreamz

Ilustraciones por
Sky Owens

la saga en curso de lecciones de vida, a través de los ojos de un niño

Traducido por
Rosie Vigiani
"TCC"
Roze Petalz

Amo A Mi Hoodie
Published by Dumplinz Book Publishing
BRONX, NY 10467
(917) 642-5549
hopesyndreamz@optonline.net
www.dumplinzbookpublishing.com

ALL RIGHTS RESERVED

No part of this book may be reproduced or transmitted in any form or by any means—electronic or mechanical, including photocopying, recording or by any information storage and retrieval system without written permission from the authors, except for the inclusion of brief quotations in a review. Requests for permission or further information should be addressed to "The Permissions Department", hopesyndreamz@optonline.net

Dumplinz Books are available at special discounts for bulk purchases, sales promotions, fund raising or educational purposes. For details, contact: Special Sales Department, Dumplinz Book Publishing, (917) 642-5549 / hopesyndreamz@optonline.net

Text Copyright © 2013 by Dumplinz Book Publishing
Illustrations Copyright © 2013 by Sky Owens
ISBN #: 978-0- 9964684-1-1
Library of Congress Control Number: 2015917838

DEDICATION

This book is humbly and graciously dedicated to Rosie Vigiani "TCC" Roze Petalz without whose undying and unending dedication to meticulous proofreading and layout...this version of Hoodie would not have been at all possible.

I love you Rosie...for being you in every way possible.

This Book is dedicated to the Memory of Trayvon Martin

and my mother, Juanita "Mommie" Wheeler....who taught me every lesson I've incorporated in my life as a woman, and who always had faith in me...always.

¡Salto de la cama!
Ayeee...pero tengo que estar tranquilito...

...o ella va a pensar que soy demasiado joven para seguir sus reglas.

Lavarse muy bien, y cepillar todos sus dientes. No se puede ser apestoso cuando estás en la calle. {ji-ji-ji}

¡Cepille, enjuague, escupa y después repita otra vez...

...si quieres que tu aliento huela a

CIIIEEELLLOOOO!!!

Voy a mi closet, por los pantalones y camisa.
¡Me pongo una media y brinca, brinca, brinca!!

Me pongo mis tenis, agarro mi abrigo y mi gorrito.

¡Tiempo para el desayuno...
...ahora si- ahí es donde está!

Tocino de pavo, huevos, tostadas con mantequilla y jugito. Ahora esta mañana está resultando ser muy bien.

Mami me sonríe y dice: *"Ya estás listo...no cabe duda. ¡Esistes mi trabajo muy fácil, ahora podemos salir!"*

Ella me agarra de la mano y por dentro...sonrio. Entramos en el carro, y nos lleva a dar una vuelta.

Sigue para abajo hasta llegar a la Calle Favor, haz una izquierda en Steinway. A cinco cuadras, haz una derecha, hacia la autopista.

Los carros pasan volando, luego nuestro carro los alcanza. Tenemos que salirnos en la salida siguiente. ¡Haga una derecha por favor!

Ella señala para virar, y los carros reducen su velocidad. Entramos en el carril derecho, y nos vamos zumbando por la calle.

La rampa de salida es larga; da vuelta y se retuerce. ¡Ayee...pero mira adelante... es la gran tienda "FITZ'S!"

Mami se estaciona en un espacio agradable.

Cerramos el carro, y caminamos hacia el lugar.

Mami me mira a mis ojos y dice, "¿Ahora, donde deberíamos empezar?" Ligeramente, como un rayo, tres muchachitos pasan corriendo.

La madre de los niños gritó: "¡muchachitos vuelvan acá!" Y rapidito ellos se agacharon detrás de los bastidores.

"¡AYE...DIOS MIOOO! QUÉ VERGÜENZA!"

Ella respirando profundamente, corría, a toda prisa para encontrarlos. Pero ellos seguían corriendo. Mami me susurró y me dijo:

"¡Aye, esto es una vergüenza! No es el momento ni el lugar, para jugar juegos tontos."

Yo le ayude aguantar ropa. Caminamos a la cajera; la primera que alcanzamos ver. La tienda estaba zumbando con ruido muy fuerte, y gente muy molesta. Pero seguimos felices-sin decir una palabra. Encontramos a una señora aburrida con pantalón azul desvanecido, ignorando a los niños que tiraban montones de ropa.

Llegamos al mostrador y colocamos nuestra ropa encima. La Dama Aburrida empieza la registradora y de repente...se detuvo...

¡AHEM!!

¡Miró a mami, y luego se aclara la garganta con fuerza, diciendo...

"¿¡QUÉ ES LO QUE VA A SER- CRÉDITO, DINERO EN EFECTIVO... TARJETA?!"

Pero mami serena, le dio una sonrisa.
Colocó su cartera en el mostrador,
mientras buscaba por un rato.

Mami buscó y buscó, su rostro se puso ceñudo. "*Ahora ¿dónde está mi cartera?*" ¡Todas sus esperanzas se empañaron! Entonces la cajera soltó un fuerte suspiro.

"¡MIRE SEÑORA...OTROS ESTÁN ESPERANDO CON COSAS PARA COMPRAR!"

"HAAAAAY!!!"

Uh Oh!

Mami se detuvo en su pánico,
y le dio un ojo agudo...
esa señora dejó de hablar, y le dio a mami más tiempo.

12

Extendiendo su mano, el habló con mami. Mientras se agitaba, dijo:
"Soy el dueño de la tienda, Tom."

"Me alegro de que eligió FITZ'S para las compras de su hijo. El es un buen chico por no correr salvaje."

Mi mami sonrió y me dio un apretón de mano... se sintió muy orgullosa.
"Pues gracias señor amable, ambos le agradecemos muchísimo. Debemos enseñar a nuestros hijos a comportarse como tal."

"Su gesto de buen corazón significa mucho para mí."
Al recompensarnos, mi mami se llenó de alegría.
"Ha crecido mucho este año, en altura. Una recompensa de vestuario, un nuevo regalo que se a ganado."
"Puedo ver que el es una joya, y para esta rara ocasión, tengo un pequeño regalo, en la estación de cajera."

Yo no lo podía creer, todo salió bien. ¿Pero porque?
Yo sólo obedecí a mami, ella nunca pide mucho.

Durante nuestro tiempo entero, mis modales me importaron. No estuve con travesuras, no era tiempo de juego.

No jugué 'persigueme por toda la tienda', avergonzandola en público, asiendo que mami se sientiera triste.

Si tomé su mano, lo único fue, que por poquito me caigo del cansancio mientras ella compraba JiJi. Pero, caminaba cuando ella caminaba, y me detuve, cuando ella se detuvo.

Para ir al baño le preguntaba, '¿me puedes llegar mami por favor?' Y cuando terminaba mi negocio...¡haaaay que alivio!

Esos muchachitos por allá, siguen cabriando sin final.
Ellos me invitan a jugar...pero nosotros no somos amigos.

"...'Sí...Señor O'Brien.'"

"Señora...Pido disculpas por mis modales. Sé que no es excusa, pero es solo uno de esos días."

"Entiendo" dijo mami, "pero por favor piensalo bien. Nos gusta venir aquí, y tenemos días malos también."

"A nuestro hijo le hemos enseñado que no importa su estado de ánimo, uno debe demostrarle a la gente respeto, no se debe ser grosero."

"*Lo siento niñito,*" ella me dijo-mientras me daba palmaditas en la cabeza.

"*Esta disculpa esta bastante tarde, así que, aquí está paletita de uva en su lugar.*"

Así que...con agradecimiento y esta paletita de uva deliciosa, nos marchamos. Mientras caminamos, dimos la vuelta y vimos la cara sonriente de la Señora Sarah.

Me encanta toda mi ropa nueva, ahora tengo ropa *para vestir*, y ahora no tengo que usar mis *pantalones* altos en el aire.

Ji-Ji

Acknowledgement

When first I sat to write this story, there never came a time when I actually had to sit and think, for long periods of time as to what exactly it was I was about to write. Words and images flow freely in that empty space some refer to lovingly as a brain…so there's really nothing up there but space and opportunities. I've loved writing as a child, and I don't think I've ever been given a topic I couldn't imagine my way through…lol. Yeah…a lot of imagination goes a long…long… LONG way. I've always loved reading stories, and telling stories to my friends, and family.

Constantly being called overly dramatic whenever I would speak was not any fun for a child…for the child within me. I took it personally, and to heart at times, lashing out whenever I accepted it as an attack. But in the grand scheme of things, I've come to realize that being called a drama queen merely caused my talents to catalytically grow, developing into the "me" I am today. So to the masses I say…"BRING ON THE DRAMA!!!"

I'm a talkative person to the umpteenth power…and all of my friends and family know this to be true. At the tender age of five, they used to run away and hide whenever they saw me coming. I always came heavily strapped with my unending arsenal of questions, scenarios, what ifs, whys, why nots, I thinks, but I thoughts, and a long string of how comes…and everyone knew it.

That leads me to this book…my first children's book ever published…to date. "I Love My Hoodie." This book was written years ago, and placed on my back shelf. I thought this was as good as any time to bring it to the forefront. With so much going on about hoodies, and crime…I thought the "hoodie" was getting a bad rep, not to mention the lads and lassies donning such attire. Something had to be done about a vital piece of clothing which has shielded us for so many decades without reproach…until now.

This was not my intent when I first wrote this piece, as the hoodie was not under a microscope, as it is today. However, it is that very thing which gave rise to my decision of releasing this story now as opposed to earlier, or later even. I wanted the little lads, and lassies out there to take note of a piece of protective clothing that cannot cause possible demise, but an item of clothing that can bring a smile to a person's face, especially when it is received as a gift from someone.

Had it not been for so many people, so many instances in my life, and so many blessings...this book would not have been possible. I thank my God, Jehovah for blessing me with the ability, the Imagination, and the stick-to-itiveness to create, to jot down on paper, and not stop until it was completed. I thank Him for life, for mommie, and daddie, for my sister Ibaria, who has never left my side, not even for an instant when mommie became ill. When the lot of my family walked away for whatever their reasons...Ibaria stayed by my side until the very end...thanks "Nikki", I'll never ever forget you for that...even if you weren't my sister, I'd appoint you as one just for that reason alone. I love you.

I thank my artist/friend/business partner brother Preston "Sky" Owens for being there for me, when all others tucked tail and ran, or just simply walked away and didn't look back...not once. I thank him for being my go-to artist in my time of need for artwork, my time of need for a listening "nerdy" ear, and for being my everlasting go-to-guy for all things comic, Photoshop, and idea bounce-er-off-er. He is the only gentleman to do all of the artwork on this... our first book together. Thank you Sky...for being that never ending little engine that "DOES". Thanks Bruh...I love you boo boo.

I thank my neighbor/sister/friend Rosie Vigiani TCC "Roze Petalz" for painstakingly translating I Love My Hoodie into "Spanglish." Not Spanish, as some may rightfully assume...but the strong fiery native Latin language of New York..."Spanglish." The language known by every child searching for their own independence, feverishly carving their own niche in the tree of life, and growing into their own form of hood-be it woman or man. I thank Rosie for keeping it as close to her childhood "Spanglish" as possible.

This is her first adventure as a translator of children's books, and in my professional opinion…she has done an incredible job of making my book come to life again but this time in "Spanglish" for every Latin child across the world. Her diligence was one for the books. She would go over the book, and go over the book until it was correct. She made sure to dot every "I" and cross every "T" before giving it to me. And after giving it to me, she would take it back before giving it to me again. This went on for a while…but I completely understood. She cares about her work, and wants nothing short of a perfect hand off every time. I appreciate that…and I appreciate "you" Roze for being the type of translator the entire world deserves.

I thank my cousin Oscar Berkley Jr., for always being the strong-minded individual he has always been - Mommie's favorite nephew. The only man in mommie's life who came to the hospital every single day, making sure I had something to eat, and a break from mommie's side for restroom antics, and the occasional wash up. For making me laugh out loud, long and hard, when every fiber in me wanted to scream out, and for showering me with that "Family Love." I'll never forget you for that dear loving cousin. I love you like cooked food.

Mommie passed away knowing she had a home. A house that she paid for, and it was transformed into a beautiful place of dwelling via the professional tutelage of our cousin. I thank my cousin Michael Wheeler, for all he did in making mommie's last memories of her home a very happy reality. For keeping that smile on her face throughout the contracting work, and for never giving up on us, despite obvious obstacles, and for seeing it through to its fruition, and for keeping me in the loop every step of the way. I thank you cousin…and I love you dearly.

I thank my best friend, Carphetis "Peaches" Aiken. Wow…where do I begin? Ok…let me just say these few words about my best friend, my long arms, my shoulders, my eyes, my back, my knees, and my incentive. Let me just thank her for being there when all hope in me was fading fast. When the spirit of writing was oozing out of my left ear…she kept my thoughts inside by stopping up my right ear. She was there…when I was tired and couldn't find the strength to fight when mommie died in 2011 from Alzheimer's.

All was possible due to Jehovah's blessings, Nikki's constant larger than life assistance, and Peaches' never-ending hands holding tight onto the slither of hope dwindling quickly within me. Because of her physical presence before me every day…I was able to keep standing on my feet. When I felt my writing was junk, she'd brow beat her devoted groupie-ness into me, with her constant pom-pom cheers. Those cheers kept me focused. For this and countless more…I thank you Peaches, for being you. "I did say 'a few words' right? Oh well…see…talkative is my middle name."

I thank my surroundings; past, present and future, the sad times, the glad times, the very bad times, the drab times, the mad times, and even those "I've been had" times in my life. I thank my bumps-cuts-and bruises, my surgeries, my stitches, my unforgettable wounds, and the wounds I deliberately forgot.

I thank the happy times, the exciting times, the abusive times, the sweetest of times, the poorest of times, the homeless times, and the affluent times. I thank my dreams, my faith, my tears, my anger, my frustrations, my curiosities, my realization, and my loves. I thank my friends, my enemies, strangers, passersby, neighbors, store owners, train/bus/plane engineers, drivers, pilots, farm animals and small machinery. I thank my abusers, and my lovers. I thank my doctors, nurses, bandages, asthma pumps, nebulizers, antibiotics, and pain killers.

In conclusion, I hope this book brings back the desire to read to our children at night, to hug and kiss them before they go to sleep, and to teach them that even when we find ourselves at our busiest moments, our darkest hours, and our saddest of times…"SOMETIMES"…all we need is to be held close and told a story. I know it

About The Team

AUTHOR: ISREBA WHEELER aka HOPE SYNDREAMZ has loved writing ever since she was in elementary school. At that time she was into poetry, and won a few poetry contests in school. Soon after, Isreba began to write stories for all of the children to read. The teachers told Isreba that her writing was over the heads of her classmates and when she got older, maybe then she should pursue writing as a career, but not now. So Isreba stopped writing...until she was an adult. Isreba joined a magazine staff for a while, but shortly thereafter connected with Illustrator Sky Owens and created Dumplinz Books.

Whenever Isreba is asked what inspired her to write children's books, she states, "Entertaining the vulnerable tiny fresh minds of our children today. Too much of life's negativity and nonsense trickles down into their bowls of cereal and they are forced to eat it up along with life's innocent lessons. I wanted to bring some morals and fun back into the eyes of these children, our children. I wanted to open up their mind's eye again, and help them recapture the essence of imagination." Isreba added, "I hope one day my children's books will inspire a child to sit me down when I am old and grey...make up a story off of the top of their heads, and tell me a story."

Isreba currently resides and works in Bronx, New York.

ILLUSTRATOR: PRESTON SKYLAR OWENS aka SKY OWENS first put crayon to paper at the tender age of 3, inspired by his mother and greatest fan. An avid fan of cartoons and comic books, he followed his passion for all of his life, working for such companies of Marvel, DC, and Dark Horse as a ghost artist, until he caught his first break as a solo artist with Fantagraphic comix, Antarctic Press, Lost Cause Production, London Night Studios until he finally self-published under Box Press and finally Action Bunny Comix. Self-taught from the beginning, he now uses the classic art methods of pencil, pen & ink, furthering his abilities with computer augmentations, bringing a new life to his illustrations. He now works and resides in a small town in New Jersey, enjoying his craft, bringing many creators' ideas to light.

TRANSLATOR: ROSIE VIGIANI aka "ROZE PETALZ" translated *I Love My Hoodie* into "Spanglish." Not Spanish, as some may rightfully assume...but the strong fiery native Latin language of New York..."Spanglish." ***Amo A Mi Hoodie*** is Rosie's first translated book, written with precision to keep it as close to her childhood "Spanglish" as possible.